Ben the Bubble Bear

Ben the **b**ear loved to blow **bubb**les.

He blew **b**ig **b**u**bb**les with blue **b**u**bb**le gum.

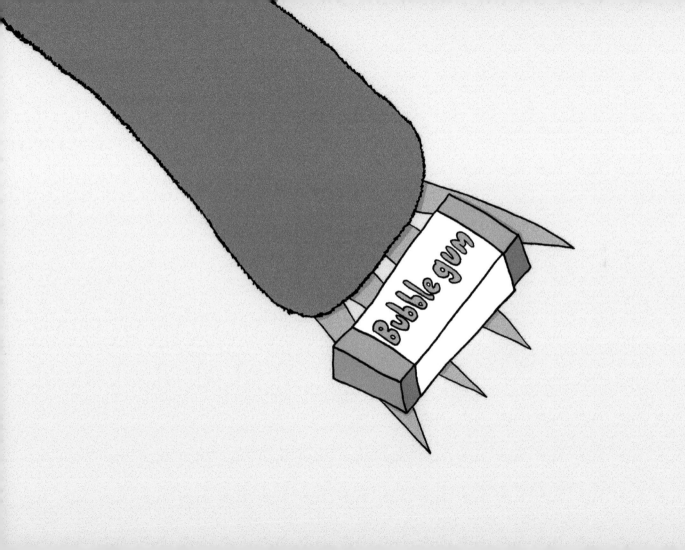

Ben blew a **bu**bble

-b-b-b-b-b-b-b-b-b-b-b-b-b-

BANG!

The **bubb**le popped! **B**en sucked the
bu**bb**le gum **b**ack into his mouth.

Along came **B**en's friend, Cale**b** the **b**ear.

"**B**en! You blow such **b**ig **bubb**les! Can you blow the **b**iggest **bubb**le in the world?" asked Cale**b**.

So **B**en blew and blew

-b-b-b-b-b-b-b-b-b-b-b-b-b-

And blew some more

-b-b-b-b-b-b-b-b-b-b-b-b-b-

Ben blew and blew even more

-b-b-b-b-b-b-b-b-b-b-b-b-b-b-b-b-

And blew the **b**iggest **b**u**bb**le Cale**b** had ever seen!

BANG! The **bubb**le exploded!

The sticky **bubb**le gum covered **B**en's face.
He couldn't get the **bu**bble gum off!

Now **B**en's face is blue like his **bu<u>bb</u>**le gum and all the **b**ears call him '**B**en the **bu<u>bb</u>**le **b**ear'!